# Reconciliation
## Prayers of Healing and Forgiveness

## —A Youth Ministry Handbook—

### Bob Grgic

**Sheed & Ward**

Sheed & Ward™ is a service of National Catholic Reporter Publishing Company Inc.

ISBN: 1-55612-422-8

Published by: Sheed & Ward
             115 E. Armour Blvd. P.O. Box 419492
             Kansas City, MO 64141-6492

To order, call: (800) 333-7373

# Contents

## Reconciliation

# Introduction

The prayer experiences contained in *Prayers of Forgiveness and Healing*, are a result of the numerous workshops and prayer experiences that I have had the honor of celebrating with many Religious Education groups of adults and youth.

The participants who have touched my life with the Lord's love, as well as you and your group, are in my prayers. I pray that the Lord of Living Waters will wash love, peace, healing and strength over you and all the people in your life.

I also pray that you allow the love of Jesus to flow through you as you minister to others. Remember, let God be God. All we need to do is be open to the Spirit, do our best, and allow God to do the rest.

May the Lord's love be realized in your friends and families as these relationships develop and deepen. The Lord is there when two or more gather in the Lord's Name. Be bathed in the Lord's love as you gather with your friends and family in the Lord's Name.

May God's love surround you and permeate every aspect of who you are.

May God's healing well up in every cell, memory, and thought.

May God's peace harmonize you with all of creation.

Bob Grgic
Creative Prayer Ministries
P.O. Box 2136
Painesville, Ohio

# Before You Begin

Many youth/adult religious education programs are using a workshop format in their catechesis. This text offers three workshop/prayer experiences which have been used with a wide variety of participants.

The workshop/prayer experiences may be used in sequence as they appear in the text, separately, or adapted to fulfill the needs of your group. You may adapt the experiences by combining meditation, journaling, and the closing prayer service of several workshop/prayer experiences.

The text can be used as a ready made 'lesson plan' with script and journal pages or as a resource from which modified prayer experiences are developed.

The flexibility of the text allows you to bring *Life* to each prayer service. As you and the planning team bring your own relationships with the Lord to the prayer experience, you speak to the hearts of the participants. As you remain open to the Spirit, the Spirit will provide an encounter with self, others, and the Lord, which will be remembered for a long time.

## Needs Assessment

Before you begin to consider which activities you are going to use, it is essential to know the needs of the group.

There are many ways to assess the needs of the group. You may wish to have a discussion asking the participants which topics are important to them. You may already have an idea of the group's needs from previous activities, discussions, retreats, etc. Or you may wish to use the 'Needs Assessment' questionnaire which is found at the end of this section (see pages xiv, xv).

After needs are identified, you may wish to ask an 'expert' to address the group on a specific subject. Some examples might be: eating disorders, drug and alcohol abuse, sexual abuse, divorce, death and grieving. After the 'facts' of dealing with these areas of need are addressed, a prayer experience 'follow up' will help the participants to place their needs in the Lord's hands.

## Choosing a Workshop/Prayer Experience

After identifying the needs of your group, look at the *Topical Index* at the end of the text. This index will help you to locate a prayer experience which fits the specific needs of your group.

If you are in need of a certain activity, you may wish to check the *Activity Index*.

If you have a certain scripture in mind and hope to find a prayer activity that corresponds to that scripture, please refer to the *Scripture Index*.

[At the end of the text there is a *Topic Index* which will refer you to the other volumes of *Prayers of Forgiveness and Healing*.]

## Maps and Options

Each group is unique. No single program, lesson, or experience will fulfill the specific needs of every group. Assess the needs of your group, use experiences which address those needs, copy all of the journal pages for the experience to adapt the experience as you go along. Many needs surface as you 'get into' an experience.

You may wish to use the experiences in this book as maps. Use the options available in the experiences but do not feel trapped by them. Allow the Spirit of God to direct your heart as you listen to the needs of the group. Modify, adapt, change whatever you feel is necessary to address the specific needs of your group.

May the Lord's Spirit flow through you as you open your heart to those in your care. May the Lord guide you as you search for options to use with your group.

# Prayer Experience Structure and Explanations

## Preparation

1. Do a Needs Assessment.

2. Choose a Prayer Experience which fits one of the needs.

3. Prepare needed materials in advance. Copy all Journal Materials. [See note on Maps and Options on page vii.]

4. Inform participants if they need to bring anything with them to the prayer experience. Use word-of-mouth by reminding participants at meetings, write up a short reminder in church bulletin, or send out postcards.

5. Set up the prayer space and prepare the environment before the group arrives.

6. Have materials ready to be passed out before the group arrives.

7. Know how the materials will be passed out:

   a. Will several volunteers pass out materials?

   b. Will you pass out materials around the circle from 2 directions and ask each participant to 'take one'?

8. When you are ready to begin the prayer experience, walk around and ask small groups of participants gathered, to join you in the large group circle.

9. Pray at every step of the preparation stage and during the prayer experience itself that all those participating will be open to the Spirit. You may even wish to ask for prayer support from other members of your church community during the preparation stage and on the night of the prayer experience.

## Prayer Experience at a Glance

This section provides an outline for the prayer experience. Those who are planning the experience may use this tool to overview the following for each prayer experience:

Suggested Time
Objectives
Introduction
Environment Suggestions
Materials Needs
Helpful Hints
Music Suggestions
Procedure Overview
After Meditation Suggestions
Evaluation/Notes
Scripture Suggestions
Topics Discussed
Activities Used

The *Prayer Experience at a Glance* section also serves as a checklist in preparing for the prayer experience. It has been helpful for planners in ordering materials, preparing copies of the journal pages, as well as preparing the environment of the 'prayer space'.

The *Prayer Experience at a Glance* section is followed by *Procedure Detailed*, which gives specific suggestions for the prayer experience as well as a 'script' which may be used.

## Time Suggestions

The time suggestions for each section is an estimate. It may take a larger group more time to complete activities then a smaller group. Be flexible in your planning. See suggestions for individual prayer experiences as well as the large and small group suggestions below.

## Group Size

Many youth/adult religious education programs use a large group model (20 or more participants) in which the participants gather together for some type of communal workshop presentation or prayer experience. After the presentation to the large group, the participants break into smaller discussion groups (10-12 participants) to process the material.

The prayer experiences in this text use this large group / small group format (but you can adapt the experiences to fit your needs). We often begin in large group, move to small group for discussion, and return to the large group for a closing prayer.

## Large Groups

We have worked with large groups (youth as well as adults) ranging in size from 20 to 200 participants. The larger the group, the greater the challenge.

Here are some suggestions which will help you to eliminate as many distractions as possible, as well as provide your participants with a meaningful prayer experience.

The larger the group, the more time you will need to allow for activities such as passing the basket to collect petitions, anointing, and laying on of hands. Most of the prayer experiences have suggestions in the section headed "Helpful Hints." These suggestions will help you to prepare for dealing with a large group and the challenges which a large group presents.

Have your materials prepared well in advance. Know how you will distribute materials to the group in an orderly manner. This will help to maintain a peaceful atmosphere.

Be certain that volunteers, group leaders, aids, etc. know what they are expected to do. It is helpful to give them any copies of discussion questions, activities, etc., well before the prayer experience. In this way, they can prepare themselves for the prayer experience and discussion time.

Keep things moving. Know what you are going to do next. Your confidence in yourself, and in the Spirit helps the group to have confidence in what you are asking them to do. Allow the Spirit to work through all you do.

As always, pray before you do anything and ask the Spirit to be present during every stage of your preparation and celebration of the prayer experience.

### Small Groups

We have also worked with small groups (both youth and adults) ranging in size from 3 to 20 participants. Groups of less than 10 participants can also be a challenge.

As for special considerations for small groups, the time factor will be the greatest. It will take the small group less time to complete any group activity or discussion. Also, the interaction of the participants as well as the dynamics of group process may be weaker in a group of less than 10 or 12 members.

Again, have your materials prepared well in advance. This will help in preventing the 'last minute rush' for the items that you wish to use in the prayer experience.

As always, pray before you do anything. Ask the Spirit to be with you and work through you and your group.

### Environment

To help set the tone of the prayer experience, have the environment set *before the participants arrive.* The prayer rug should be set, the lights should be lowered to the level you desire, and some soft music should be playing. This will help the participants to enter the experience as soon as they enter the room.

### Relaxation / Meditation Experience

*Suggestions for teens only.*

You may wish to ask the *teens* to move from the circle and to sit about ten feet from each other before the meditation begins. This seems to eliminate some of the distractions which 'peer pressure' tends to foster. If certain youths have a difficult time relaxing or do not wish to participate in this type of experience, you may gently walk up to the individuals causing the disruption and offer them an option.

You may offer them an optional experience in another room. I have offered the following optional lesson to teens many times. But seldom have I had a teen choose this option.

Tell them, "I'm sorry if this experience is not fulfilling the needs that you have at this time. If you would like to join Mr./Ms._____ in another room and discuss the material that we are going to cover, please join them now in room _____ , or you may remain here with us. But please do not disturb anyone else . . ."

Be sure that you have a room and a moderator for those who choose this optional prayer experience. These arrangements should be made in advance. There the participants may discuss the Journal pages as well as the discussion questions for the prayer experience.

The Relaxation experience is the same for each meditation. This tensing and relaxing of muscles is very effective in relaxing the individuals. If you use this technique more than 3 times, you may wish to ask the participants to slow down their breathing, relax their facial area, arms, and legs.

The meditations are different but convey an atmosphere in which the participants may talk with the Lord. Some of the meditations are variations on a theme. The idea is to help the participants to gain a sense of peacefulness. The meditations are set in an arrangement to help the participants move from one idea to another. They need not be used in the order given.

### Gathering Prayer Requests

Often times the participants are asked to write down a prayer request, 'hurt,' or some other 'need' which they wish to offer to the Lord. Most of the times they are asked to take the request (which is usually written on a small piece of paper) and rip it up. Then they are asked to place it in a basket which is passed around the group.

You may ask the participants in a smaller group to share their petition if they feel that they would like the group to pray for a specific intention. *Never force participants to share in the small group.*

If they would like to remain quiet, they may remain silent as they place their petition in the basket. Either way, ask the members of the group to pray for each person as they place their request in the basket.

If your group is larger than 25 to 30 participants, you may wish to have two baskets to pass around the circle in different directions. This cuts down on the amount of time needed to collect the petitions and helps the participants to prayerfully focus on what is going on.

The drawback to the multiple-basket option is that the participants cannot share as easily their petitions with the group if they wish to do so. Also, it is difficult for participants to pray for each person placing their petition in the basket if multiple baskets are being used.

An alternative for gathering petitions in a large group would be to ask participants to remain in their small groups. After the discussion time collect the petitions in the small groups. This allows the participants the opportunity to share their petitions if they wish to do so.

For other suggestions, see the Helpful Hints sections which preface each prayer experience.

## *Journal Pages*

You may wish to invite the participants to keep the journal pages used during the prayer experiences in a special folder. This does not have to be anything fancy, but it should be used only for prayerful reflection. This will help the participants to focus on what they are praying for and will help reduce distractions.

Treat journal materials as confidential. Do not ask participants to read from their journals. Rather ask for any insights that participants may have gained from the introduction to the theme, the meditation, or journal experience.

If your program is financially able to provide the participants with the prayer journal folders, this will be a gesture that the participants will appreciate.

If your program can not cover the cost of the folders, then just ask the participants to bring in a 'three ring' folder which will be used for the journal pages. Again, stress that we will only use the journal for prayer times.

Some people find it helpful to keep a daily journal. Some find it helpful to write a letter to the Lord each day. They find that the letter format helps them to focus on their prayer. You may wish to copy some of the blank letter starters (see page xiv) and include several copies in the journal folders when they are passed out.

It may be helpful to copy all of the journal pages for a specific prayer experience. This will give you the flexibility to move into an area of need which arises during the experience. [For further details see Maps and Options page vii.]

## *Small Group Discussion*

This is a very powerful time for the participants. Some may wish to share their insights with the group, while others may wish to sit quietly and listen. It is important that individuals feel that they may share if they wish or remain quiet if they wish. Help the participants to understand that they do not have to share their feelings if they feel uncomfortable doing so. They may 'pass' if they wish.

If a person shares his/her feelings and is in visible need of prayer, ask the Holy Spirit to be present. When the person is finished sharing, ask them if they would like to pray with the group.

Ask the group to join hands and to pray for the person who has just shared his/her story. The leader may wish to lay hands (see page xi) while the group prays silently or aloud for the person.

**Consistent Group Membership:** You may wish to use small groups in which the membership is chosen by the leaders and remains consistent each time the group meets. One way to tell the participants which group they belong to is by color coding name tags. Invite each color to meet in small groups. Or you may wish to ask participants to choose their own groups and to remain in the same grouping each time small groups are used.

The consistent small groups helps the participants to build community. They will begin to know the other group members and may feel free to talk openly and honestly.

**Inconsistent Group Membership:** Allow the participants to choose their own groups consisting of 10 - 12 members. Each time the group meets, the participants will be asked to gather in groups of 10 - 12 (membership will not be the same each time the group meets). This type of group will consist of people who most likely know each other already.

One drawback to the 'inconsistent membership' type of group is that the 'trust factor' may not be as strong in a group which changes membership each time it meets as it would if the group had consistent membership. On the other hand, a drawback to 'consistent membership' is that, when participants choose their own group they may not meet new people who are outside of their usual circle of friends.

## Anointing

As a closing prayer, anointing with water or oil is often used. This consists of asking the group to pray over the water or the oil, and then passing the water/oil around the circle. One person at a time makes the Sign of the Cross on the person to their right's forehead (or palms of hands). A short prayer (silent or aloud) may be said as the Sign of the Cross is made.

In a large group (more than 25-30 participants) you may wish to have two containers of water/oil for anointing in the circle. This will shorten the time needed for the anointing and help the group to focus on praying for those being anointed, without becoming tedious.

## Laying on of Hands

This is a special way to pray for each other. The prayer experiences which use this prayer form will explain the procedure for its use with the specific prayer experience.

In general, the group leader will move from one person to the next, going around the circle, laying his/her hands on the head or shoulders of each participant.

The leader will ask the Spirit to flow through him/her and into the person for which he/she is praying. The leader may think of himself/herself as a pipeline of God's love, forgiveness, and healing.

The leader may wish to ask each individual he/she comes to "Is there anything special that you would like to pray for today?" The individual may wish to tell the leader what it is that he/she would like to pray for or may wish to remain silent.

The leader may experience some insight into whatever it is he/she should pray for. The Lord may grant some insight into the area which the person is in need of prayer. Take this as a gift and if you feel the Lord wishes you to talk with the participant privately after the service, please do this.

You may wish to ask "Is there anything you would like to talk about?" Again, pray about this and allow the participant the freedom to say, "No, I really would rather not talk about this right now." If they do not wish to talk about it, assure the participant that you will continue to pray for them and whatever it is that they are dealing with.

A 'warm, tingling feeling' may be experienced as the Laying on of Hands prayer is entered into. This may or may not be felt. Sometimes God gives us warm 'hugs' and we experience this feeling. What matters is that *you reach out to another in God's love,* allow the Spirit to flow through you, and genuinely care about another person. Ask God's Spirit to flow through you and fill the life of the person for which you are praying.

## Fellowship Time

This is a time which allows the participants to continue to give support to each other. It is also a time for the participants to grow as a community.

Your program may be able to absorb the cost of refreshments, or you may wish to ask the participants to bring some type of refreshments to the meeting. This also helps as a 'buffer', in case the time of the prayer experience runs a few minutes over or under the expected time. If the time runs over, those who have to leave right away can leave and those who can remain may stay and have fellowship. If the time runs a little under what you expected, the participants have the opportunity to spend more time with one another in an atmosphere which offers support and friendship.

## New Age Cautions

'New Age' literature and materials use relaxation, guided meditation techniques, and even Laying on of Hands. One of the many problems is that they do not focus on the Lord in their experiences.

Be sure to tell the participants that the techniques used in this text are not New Age but rather experiences which are centered on the Lord being Lord and on the participants calling on the Spirit of God to fill their lives.

None of the tapes used should have any subliminal messages. (Subliminal messages are encoded on some relaxation tapes bought through magazines, record stores, or in drug stores. The message encoded is not audible to your conscious mind, but the subconscious can pick it up. The message is often 'Relax' or 'You are a good person' or some other positive message.)

The tapes recommended in this text are free from any subliminal messages. Be sure to tell the participants that you are using relaxation music that does not contain such messages.

One group of youth that I ministered to had a teenage boy who was into occult activities. He wanted to know if we were going to, "turn off the lights and go into a trance." I told him, "No!  We are going to talk with the Lord tonight and invite Jesus into our hearts." Instead of turning down the lights for the meditation, we kept the lights on. We still did the guided meditation, but I kept stressing that this was a relaxed state. We were meeting the *Lord* in meditation.

There are a number of good books out on the New Age and what to watch out for. It may be a good idea to read as much as you can. In this way you will know what to look out for and what to avoid.

Be sure to ground everything that you do in the Lord's Name and in the Spirit. With God as your focus, what you do will be done in a prayerful way and in the Lord's Spirit.

## Symbols

Not all of the following symbols are used at one time.  See the individual prayer experiences for specific items used on the prayer rug. Specific suggestions for items used on the prayer rug are found under the sections titled: *Prayer Service at a Glance*, Materials Needed, as well as the *Procedure Detailed*, Part I.

The *Prayer Rug* provides a focal point. It is a space where special objects and written prayer requests are placed and prayed for.

The list which follows gives suggestions for items used on the prayer rug.

The Prayer Rug doesn't have to be anything fancy, but should be used only for prayer. If it has to be returned to the kitchen floor, it tends to 'lose something' in the eyes of the participants.

A rug which is approximately 2'x4' would be sufficient in size. As for the color and design of the rug, find something which looks like it will help to create a prayerful atmosphere.

*Incense* reminds us that our prayers (like the smoke) rise up to the Lord. Find a scent that you enjoy and which is not too 'heavy'.

The incense can be the type that a drug store sells or you may wish to use church incense. I have found that the 'cone' type incense has a pleasant aroma and burns easily.

A ceramic 'japanese tea cup' (a small cup without a handle) or some other small ceramic container works well to place the incense in. Be careful to place the incense cone on a small brass three legged holder (usually available where they sell incense) which separates the hot incense from the bottom of the cup. An inch of sand may also be used instead of the brass holder. The sand will absorb the heat of the incense.

If the brass holder or sand are not used, the bottom of the cup gets very hot and may turn the prayer rug a 'burnt brown'. Be sure incense is completely extinguished when the service is over to avoid an accidental fire.

*Water* reminds us of our baptism.

You can use a clear 'rocks' type glass to place the water in. Fill the glass with about an inch of water and set it on the prayer rug.

When you finish the prayer service, ask one of the participants to take the water outside and pour it into the grass or soil. Ask the person pouring the water out to pray that the Lord will bless and heal the Earth.

If one of the participant's family or friends is ill, you may wish to send the water home to them in a small plastic bottle. Ask the participant to bless the person at home with the water and tell them that the prayers of the group are with them.

Just as with the rug itself, treat the water as a symbol that has special meaning. Pouring the water down the drain some place and treating the water like any old water, contradicts the sacred meaning that we have given to the symbol.

*Oil.* We are told in James 5:13-16 that when someone is sick, we should ask the presbyters of the church to pray over him/her and anoint him/her with oil in the name of the Lord.

A small glass container (similar to the style of the glass used for the water and candle) may be used in which you may place a few cotton balls. Pour a few drops of olive oil onto the cotton balls.

As with the water, do not just throw the oil and cotton away after the prayer experience. You may wish to combine the cotton with the petitions collected and then burn all of this at one time. Again, treat these items as symbols which are important to those who have used them in prayer today.

*Scripture* reminds us of the promises that the Lord has made to us. We are told of God's saving love and care for the people of the Hebrew Scripture. We are shown God's love for all people in Jesus life and the life of the early Church. Jesus loved the people who lived during his time and showed his love for them. We are told, in *Acts* and in the *Letters*, of the Spirit's love and about the healings which took place after Jesus ascended into heaven.

Place the scripture on the prayer rug open to the passage that will be used during the prayer experience.

A *Candle* reminds us that Jesus is the Light of the world. As the light pierces the darkness, so the love of God frees us from the darkness of sin in our life.

A small 'vigil light' candle placed in a rocks type glass (similar to the one that the water is in) will work well. The glass will allow the light of the candle to be seen as well as contain the hot wax.

With the candle in the glass, you can pass the candle around the circle and ask the participants to share a petition that they would like the group to pray for. The participant may also remain quiet, knowing that the group is praying for the petition that they hold in the silence of their heart.

A *Small Basket* will serve as a container to collect the petitions which will be offered to the Lord during the closing prayer.

Again, none of the items on the prayer rug need to be very expensive. Try to find items that will serve the purpose as well as help create a prayerful atmosphere.

Participants will write their prayer request on strips of paper. They will then be asked to tear up the strips of paper. This will assure them that no one reads what they have written.

When the petitions have been torn up and the basket passed to gather the petitions, tell the participants that you will burn these pieces of paper at a later time, or you may wish to burn them while the group is gathered (see note on Metal Container below).

A *Metal Container* is used to burn the petitions collected as well as the cotton balls soaked with oil. If you burn the petitions while the group is gathered, there is no need to tear them up.

The container should be approximately twelve inches deep. Fill the container with three to four inches of sand. This helps to absorb the heat of the burning paper. Place the metal container on a nonflammable surface (a good pot holder works well).

Whenever you are burning things, it is good to have a *fire extinguisher* near by.

The smell and smoke from burning paper do not add to a prayerful atmosphere. The symbolism of these requests being offered to the Lord may be very powerful for the participants, but the smell too is very 'powerful'. If you think the group would benefit from the burning of the petitions, then use this activity, but be sure windows can be opened.

If you have access to a fireplace, the burning works well because of the natural venting of the smoke. If you are in a small area with no ventilation, the smoke gets thick and others in the building think there is a real fire.

Be sure to tell others what you are doing so no one is alarmed by the smell of smoke.

## Prayer Journal

You may find it helpful to keep a prayer journal.

The following page may be helpful as it aids you to focus during your prayer time.

You are invited to write a letter to the Lord as you would write to your closest friend.

You may wish to make copies of this blank page and use it daily.

May the Lord Speak to your heart as you take time to listen.

# Journal Page

Date _____

Scripture reading
used today _____

People in need
of prayer _____

_____

_____

People who
had prayers answered _____

_____

_____

Dear Lord,

_____

_____

_____

_____

_____

_____

_____

_____

_____

_____

_____

_____

_____

_____

_____

_____

_____

_____

_____

_____

©1990, Creative Prayer Ministries, P.O. Box 2136, Painesville, Ohio 44077 *Prayers of Forgiveness and Healing*, Bob Grgic

# Youth Assessment

## *Prayers of Forgiveness and Healing*

*Please be as honest as possible when completing this needs assessment! This will help us to plan future sessions to meet your needs and the needs of the other participants.*

**Directions:** Please circle no more than three items in each section. If you do not have a need in a section, please do not circle anything for the section.

### A. Personal Forgiveness:

| | | |
|---|---|---|
| Improving Self-Esteem | Forgiving Myself | Asking God's Forgiveness |
| Quiet time with the Lord | Loving Myself | Other _____ |

### B. Family and Other Relationships:

| | | | | |
|---|---|---|---|---|
| Mom | Dad | Step Mom | Step Dad | Teacher |
| Brother | Uncle | Step Brother | Step Sister | Best Friend |
| Sister | Aunt | Romantic Friend | Boss | Enemy |
| | | | Other _____ | |

### C. In Need of Healing:

| | | |
|---|---|---|
| Emotions | Memories of Painful Events | Pain from parent's divorce |
| Nightmares | Physical Injury | Physical Injury of a Friend |
| | | Other _____ |

### D. In Need of Freedom From:

| | | |
|---|---|---|
| Sexual Abuse | Alcohol Abuse | Occult Participation |
| Over Eating | Negative habits | Satan Worship |
| Eating Disorders | Peer Pressure | Other _____ |

### E. Letting Go of:

| | | |
|---|---|---|
| Another's hurt | Anger | A habit |
| Death of a friend/ loved one | Resentment | Other _____ |

**Write in the most important need from each section:**

A. Personal _____

B. Family _____

C. Healing _____

D. Freedom _____

E. Letting Go _____

# Adult Assessment

*Please be as honest as possible when completing this needs assessment! This will help us to plan future sessions to meet your needs and the needs of the other participants.*

**Directions:** Please circle no more than three items in each section. If you do not have a need in a section, please do not circle anything for the section.

### A. Personal Forgiveness:

| | | |
|---|---|---|
| Improving Self Esteem | Forgiving Myself | Asking God's Forgiveness |
| Quiet time with the Lord | Loving Myself | Other _____ |
| Forgiveness of sins of my youth | | |

### B. Family and Other Relationships:

| | | | | |
|---|---|---|---|---|
| Mom | Dad | Step-Mom | Step-Dad | Past Teacher |
| Brother | Uncle | Step-Brother | Step-Sister | Best Friend |
| Sister | Aunt | Romantic Friend | Boss | Enemy |
| Son | Daughter | Step-Son | Step-Daughter | Ex-Spouse |
| Spouse | | Other _____ | | |

### C. In Need of Healing:

| | | |
|---|---|---|
| Emotions | Memories of Painful Events | Pain from divorce |
| Nightmares | Physical Injury | Physical Injury of a Friend |
| | Other _____ | |

### D. In Need of Freedom From:

| | | |
|---|---|---|
| Sexual Abuse | Alcohol Abuse | Occult Participation |
| Over Eating | Negative Habits | Satan Worship |
| Eating Disorders | Peer Pressure | Spouse's Choices |
| Enabling Addiction of another | A child's choice of life style | Other _____ |

### E. Letting Go of:

| | | |
|---|---|---|
| Another's hurt | Anger | A habit |
| Death of a friend/loved one | Resentment | Other _____ |
| Children's choices/Spouse's Choices | | |

#### Write in the most important need from each section:

A. Personal _____

B. Family _____

C. Healing _____

D. Freedom _____

E. Letting Go _____

# Jesus, Calm My Sea

## Suggested Time:

One Hour to One Hour and a Half

## Objectives:

1. To create an atmosphere in which the participants may relax in the Lord's love and peace.

2. To help the participants to relax their body and mind.

3. To Invite participants to ask Jesus to be with them and bring peace to specific areas in their lives.

4. To help the participants to identify areas in their lives which are in need of forgiveness and healing. They will be invited to ask Jesus to heal these areas.

## Introduction

This meditation/prayer experience invites the participants to relax their body and mind. A guided meditation will help the participants to ask Jesus to calm the storms in their lives.

This can be a very meaningful experience and has proven to be a time when the participants can talk 'face to face' with the Lord.

In your introduction to the prayer experience, you (or the person giving the witness) may wish to talk about what the Lord means to you. How is Jesus working in your life to bring you peace and healing? The more personal your reflection on Jesus, who brings forgiveness and healing, the more believable your witness will be.

It may help the participants to understand God's love for them, and their love for the Lord, by comparing a relationship to God with a relationship they have with a friend, spouse, or parent. It would be helpful if the person introducing the theme would witness to God's love and compare their love for the Lord with their love for a friend, spouse, or parent. It is good to highlight the similarities as well as the differences in God's love and a friend's love.

This meditation experience has three major movements. First the participants meet the Lord in meditation. Second, the participants receive the Lord's love as another reaches out and anoints them with the water. Third, participants meet the Lord as they reach out to the person sitting next to them and anoint them with water. (See page xi for notes on anointing.)

## Environment

We would like to set a relaxed and peaceful environment for this meditation.

Lights dimmed

Soft music playing (see music suggestions below)

Prayer rug set with:

Lit Incense

Lit Candle

Bible open to passage being used (Matt. 8: 23-27 or similar passage)

Water in small container(s) for anointing

Small Basket(s) to collect prayer petitions in.

Gather in a circle around the prayer rug.

## Materials

*Participants should bring:*

Optional:

1. Snacks for fellowship time.

2. A blanket to sit on during the meditation experience. If carpet squares are available, these may also be used. The blanket/carpet squares allow the participants to sit on the floor if they wish during the meditation experience. You may wish to have chairs available for

those who wish to sit in a chair. Know the needs and the abilities of your group. The key is to help the participants to relax.

*Leader Prepares:*

Review Preparation Notes on page viii.

> Journal Pages
> (page 8)
> Picture of Jesus
> (pocket card)
> Letter from Jesus
> Strip of Paper 2" x 8 1/2

These should be sealed into an envelope for each Letter from Jesus participant.

Copies of page 44 for the leaders of the small group discussion time.

**Kleenex**

**Pencils or pens**

**Prayer Rug,** helps to set a sense of sacred space. See page xii for more detailed explanation.

**Incense,** either a Drugstore/popular brand is fine, or church incense may also be used. See page xii for more detailed explanation.

**Water Container** for anointing. A 'rocks' glass works well or you may wish to use a small pottery vase to place the water in. See page xii for a more detailed explanation.

**Basket** for collecting petitions. See page xiii for a more detailed explanation.

**Candle**  See page xiii for a more detailed explanation.

**Scripture**  See pages xii-xiii for a more detailed explanation.

**Record/tape player**

Choose/ask for a volunteer to give a witness on Jesus calming the stormy seas in his/her life. See Introduction on page 30 for guide questions.

Choose/ask for adult volunteers to act as small group facilitators. It would be helpful to copy the questions for the small group discussion page x and give them the copies well in advance.

## Helpful Hints

You may wish to ask the participants to keep a prayer journal. This might be a loose leaf folder into which the participants can place the journal pages used during the meditation experiences. It is important that these pages be kept confidential. Please do not read the participants' journal pages, or ask them to read from them. See pages x for background on journals and small group discussion.

Before you begin the meditation, pass out all the materials that the participants will need.

Ask the participants to move from the circle and sit about ten feet apart if it looks as if they might be distracted by the others sitting around them.

> This meditation experience can be used with groups from 10-200 participants. If the group is larger than 40, you may wish to use two containers of water for anointing, and two baskets to collect petitions. Try to work out of one circle if possible. If this is not possible, have groups of about 10-12 participants make smaller circles gathered around the prayer rug. See Illustration.

## Music Suggestions

*Relaxation/ Meditation time*

*Your Heart's Prayer*, The Body at Prayer, Vol 2, Sparough and Fisher, 1987, St. Anthony Messenger

*Praise Strings,* Vol 11, Maranatha! Music, 1989

*Jonathan Livingston Sea Gull,* The Original Motion Picture Sound Track from the Hall Bartlett Film, Neil Diamond, CBS Inc. 1973

*Journal time*

*Hello*, The Jazz Singer, Neil Diamond, 1980, Capitol Records

*People Need the Lord,* Let There Be Praise Singers, 1986, Sparrow Corp.

*Reflections,* Vol. 1, 2, 3

Any quiet music which will help to set the atmosphere for meditation and reflection.

*Anointing Time*

*He Has Anointed Me, Path of Life,* Dameans

## Prayer Experience at a Glance

### Part I  (10-15 Minutes)

Gather in Circle around prayer rug

Introduce the evening's theme, reading, and witness.

Explain the prayer rug and symbols.

### Part II (3-5 minutes)

Pass out pencils and envelopes.  Don't open the envelopes yet. Please wait until you are invited to open them.

### Part III  (20 minutes)

Relaxation / Meditation

### Part IV  (10-15 minutes)

Journal Experience

### Part V  (15-20 Minutes)

Optional: small group discussion

### Part VI  (10-15 minutes)

Closing Prayer:

Placing petitions in Basket

Anointing

### Part VII  (10-15 minutes)

Optional: fellowship time (snacks )

Or open gym

## After Meditation Experience

Invite the participants to spend a few minutes each day with the Lord. Invite the Lord to be a part of their every day life.

May invite the participants to keep a prayer journal. This will help them to understand their growth in their relationship with the Lord. See page x.

## Evaluation / Notes

## Index

### Scripture

Matthew 8: 23-27

### Topics

Friendship of Jesus

Inviting Jesus into one's life

Peace, asking Jesus for

Prayer, Introduction to

Reconciliation, Recognize need for

Relaxation Techniques

### Activities

Anointing: with water on forehead

Group, Large: opening prayer

Closing Prayer

Group, Small: optional discussion

Journal, Individual prayer time

Meditation:  Pray for loved one.

Petitions: written, ripped up, placed in basket

## Procedure Detailed

### Part I  (10-15 Minutes)

**Invite participants to Gather in Circle around prayer rug.**

Introduce the evening's theme (Given by leader or a person who can witness to the love of Jesus calming the storm in their life.)  See suggestions below as well as Introduction on page v for idea starters.

a. Read or paraphrase Matt. 8:23-27

b. How do I know that Jesus cares about me?

c. How has Jesus calmed the Storms in my Life?

d. How has my relationship with Jesus deepened? How has our friendship grown?

e. How have I asked Jesus to help me with specific areas or incidents in my life?

f. How can I compare a relationship with Jesus to a relationship with a friend, spouse, or parent.

Explain the prayer rug and symbols:

**Prayer Rug,** is a focal point. It will become a place upon which we set our prayer requests. We will also set items upon the rug which we will ask the Lord to bless. (See page xii)

**Incense,** (may already be lit or light it at this point). The incense reminds us that our prayers (like the smoke) rise up to the Lord. (See page xii)

**Water,** reminds us of our baptism in Jesus' death and new life. (See page xii)

**Candle,** reminds us that Jesus is the Light of the World. We Gather in the Light of Jesus. (See page xiii)

**Scripture,** reminds us of the promises that Jesus made to us. Jesus loved the people who lived during his time and showed his love for them. Jesus loves you today and wants to show his love for you. (See pages xii-xiii)

**Small Basket,** will serve as a container to collect the petitions which will be offered to the Lord during the closing prayer. (See page xiii)

## Part II (3-5 minutes)

Pass out envelopes and pencils. Ask participants not to open them yet.

Ask teenagers to move about ten feet apart. Adults may remain in the circle. (See page ix)

## Part III (20 minutes)

**Relaxation / Meditation** (You may wish to read the script below or you may wish to adapt it to fit your needs.)

**Begin the tape, The Body at Prayer, Vol. 1,** St. Anthony Messenger, Sparough and Fisher, 1987. (Side two which has ocean sounds with music). Or Sea Shore sounds *without* subliminal messages. Any quiet music will work. (See page 2 for music suggestions.)

(Read/Adapt )

During this prayer experience we will work on relaxing our bodies and our minds. This will help us to reduce the distractions which usually occupy our attention. If there is something in your life, which is in need of help or of offering to the Lord, offer it to the Lord today. Ask the Lord who calmed the storm on the sea to calm the storm in your life.

Know that all that we do today and from this moment on will be completed in the love of Jesus. Jesus wants to calm your life and to give you the peace, healing, and forgiveness that you seek today.

(*Speak slowly and calmly. Your voice will add to the relaxing atmosphere which you have set.*)

Try to find a *comfortable position*. You may wish to sit in the chair or on a blanket on the floor. You may even wish to lay down, but a word of caution, do not get too comfortable, since you may fall asleep.

Please *close your eyes*. This will help reduce visual distractions and will help you to focus your thoughts on the Lord.

We begin to quiet our minds and bodies as we start to *slow down our breathing*.

As you inhale, slowly count to four without making any noise. (*Pause*)
As you exhale, slowly count to four without making any noise.

(*Allow participants to take about 3 or 4 breaths and continue*)

As you inhale accept the Spirit of God into your life. (*Pause*)
As you exhale let go of anything which makes you nervous or anxious.

(*Allow participants to take about 3 or 4 breaths and continue*)

As your breathing slows and calms, so will your body and mind.

(*Speak slowly and calmly. Your voice will add to the relaxing atmosphere which you have set.*)

Our next step in relaxation will be *relaxing various muscle groups*.

Beginning with your *forehead*, crinkle it up and close your eyes as tightly as you can. Feel the tension in your forehead, the corners of your eyes, and feel your nose crinkle up. Hold the tension...and then relax. Feel what it is like to be tense and relaxed.

Then hold your *lips* together as tightly as you can and *bite down* as hard as you can. Feel the tension in the corners of your mouth and in your jaw. Hold the tension . . . and then relax. Feel what it is like to be tense and relaxed.

As you inhale, slowly count to four without making any noise. (*Pause*)
As you exhale, slowly count to four without making any noise.

(*Allow participants to take about 3 or 4 breaths and continue.*)

As you inhale accept the Spirit of God into your life. (*Pause*)
As you exhale let go of anything which makes you nervous or anxious.

(*Allow participants to take about 3 or 4 breaths and continue.*)

Next, we will work on relaxing your *neck*. Allow your chin to touch your chest and begin to slowly do some neck rolls. First to the right . . . Feel the tension as you extend various muscles. . . . Then go to the left . . . and begin to work out the kinks in your neck. Now return your head to a resting position and relax. Feel what it is like to be tense and relaxed.

Now, Shrug your *shoulders*. Move them as close to your neck as you can. Feel the tension in your neck and shoulders. Then push your shoulders toward your feet. Push them away from your neck. Feel the tension under your arms, in your back and in your neck. Hold the tension . . . and then relax. Feel what it is like to be tense and relaxed.

As you inhale, slowly count to four. (*Pause*)
As you exhale, slowly count to four.

(*Allow participants to take about 3 or 4 breaths and continue.*)

As you inhale accept the Spirit of God into your life. (*Pause*)
As you exhale let go of anything which makes you nervous or anxious.

(*Allow participants to take about 3 or 4 breaths and continue.*)

Beginning with your right hand, make a fist and tighten up all the muscles in your *right arm*, forearm and biceps. Feel the tension in your right arm. Hold the tension. You may even feel your right arm quiver. Experience the tension . . . and then relax. Feel what it is like to be tense and relaxed.

Now repeat the same procedure with your Left hand. Make a fist and tighten up all the muscles in your *left arm*, forearm and biceps. Feel the tension in your Left arm. Hold the tension. You may even feel your Left arm quiver . . . and then relax. Feel what it is like to be tense and relaxed.

As you inhale, remember to count slowly to four. (*Pause*)
As you exhale, remember to count slowly to four.

(*Allow participants to take about 3 or 4 breaths and continue.*)

As you inhale accept the Spirit of God into your life. (*Pause*)
As you exhale let go of anything which makes you nervous or anxious.

(*Allow participants to take about 3 or 4 breaths and continue.*)

Beginning with your *right leg*. Curl up your foot and tighten all the muscles in your right leg, calf and thigh. Feel the tension in your right leg. Hold the tension. You may even feel your right leg quiver and it may feel like it is going to cramp. Experience the tension . . . and now relax. Feel what it is like to be tense and relaxed.

Now repeat the same procedure with your *left leg*. Curl up your foot and tighten all the muscles in your Left leg, calf and thigh. Feel the tension in your Left leg. Hold the tension. You may even feel your Left leg quiver and it may feel like it is going to cramp . . . and now relax. Feel what it is like to be tense and relaxed.

Tighten your abdomen muscles as you inhale, and allow the tension to leave you as you exhale.

Now that your body is calm and relaxed, I would ask you to think about your favorite beach.

First we will focus on the sky. (*Pause after each question.*)

What colors are the sky?
Are there clouds?
What time of day or night is it? How does that effect the sky?
What do you notice about the sky that you have never noticed before?

Next we will focus on the water.

What does the water look like?
What colors are present?
Is the water calm or choppy?
What does the water smell like?
What do you notice about the water that you have never noticed before?

Finally we will focus on the beach itself.

Look at the beach around you?
What is in or on the sand around you?
What do you see that you have never
noticed before?
Pick up a handful of sand and look at it.
What do you see that you have never
noticed before?

I would ask you at this point to walk into the water until you are about waist deep. Keep looking out to sea.

If the waves are choppy, they may try to
push you back.

As you enter the water, begin to notice that
with each breath that you take, the waves
begin to quiet until they finally become
calm.

Keep looking out over the water experienc-
ing the calm and peace of this place.

Invite Jesus onto your beach. As you turn around, you see that Jesus is standing behind you on the shore.

What do his eyes look like?
What does his face look like?
How tall is he?

(*Continue to Speak slowly and calmly. Pause in between paragraphs.*)

What do you feel as you look at him and as he extends his arms out toward you?

Jesus invites you to leave the water. As you come out of the water, Jesus embraces you. What do you tell him that you have wanted to tell him for so long, but you have never had the time or energy to tell him before?  And what is his response to you?

(*Longer Pause*)

Jesus asks you to invite a special person who gives meaning to your life onto your beach.

As this special person walks toward you, down the beach, what emotion do you experience?

Jesus walks up to the person and  embraces this person who holds such a tender spot in your heart.

What do you feel as you look at Jesus and this im-portant person?

Jesus invites you to walk over toward him and your special guest. As you move toward Jesus, he embraces you and your special person, bringing you both to-gether in Loving arms.

What do you tell this important person in your life, that you have wanted to tell him/her for so long, but you have never had the time or courage to tell them before?  And what is his/her response to you?

(*Longer Pause*)

It is time for this special person to leave and before they do, you tell them one last thing.

Your guest begins to walk down the beach. Only you and the Lord remain on the beach. Jesus embraces you. What do you talk to the Lord about.

(*Longer Pause*)

Jesus assures you that He is with you even as you open your eyes. I would invite you to open the en-velopes that you have been given and to complete the journal pages quietly on your own. Continue this time of meditation and quiet time with the Lord.

Please be honest in answering the journal ques-tions. No one will read these pages.

## Part IV  (10 - 15 minutes)

### Journal Experience  (pages xiii-xiv)

Play the song: *Hello*, by Neil Diamond, or another appropriate song. When this song is finished keep playing some quiet meditation music until journal writing is complete.

Before you regather in the circle, ask the partici-pants to:

"Please tear off and complete the small piece of paper containing your request of Jesus today. Be as honest as possible. No one will read these. We will rip them up into tiny pieces during the closing prayer to assure that no one will read them. We will then offer these requests to the Lord."

## Part V  (15 - 20 Minutes)

### Optional Small group discussion

Gather in groups of 10 - 12 with a person who has volunteered to be the facilitator.

See notes on small group discussion on page 10.

You may wish to discuss:

a. Was the relaxation technique helpful?

b. What did you find most helpful from the meditation experience?

c. What did you find least helpful?

d. What do you ask of the Lord today that you would like to share with the group for their support in prayer? *Only share what you feel comfortable sharing.* Remember that you may 'pass' if you do not wish to share your insights or thoughts.

## Part VI  (10-15 minutes)

**Closing Prayer:**

Regather in the Circle.

(*Allow a few moments for regathering.*)

Please take out the small strips of paper on which you wrote your request for the Lord to answer.

We will pass around the basket. Please rip up your request and place it in the basket. (*See notes pages ix-x.*)

If you would like to say out loud what you are asking of the Lord so that we too may join in your prayer, please say your request out loud.

If you would like to place your request in the basket silently, please do that. Know that we are still praying for your request as you silently place your request in the basket.

(*Take the basket(s) from the prayer rug and pass it around the circle. Participants place petitions in basket . . . After the basket(s) has been passed, return it to the prayer rug.*)

We will burn these ripped up petitions after our meeting today. Please take a moment to prayer for each other's petitions which we have offered to the Lord. (*Short Pause*) (*See note page xiii.*)

We have experienced the presence of God in many ways during this experience:

First through Meditation
Then through a Journal Reflection
And now through the touch of another.

We will now pray over the water which is on the prayer rug. We will ask the Lord to bless the water so that it may be a sign of God's love, peace, and healing for all those who are anointed with it.

Then we will pass the water around the circle. Each person will take the small container of water, dip their finger into the water, and make the sign of the cross on the person's forehead to their right.

We ask that the whole group pray for the person being anointed with water. Focus your attention and prayers on that one person. Ask the Lord to bless them and to grant them what is best for everyone involved.

Now please hold out your right hand over the water and we will pray.

Please repeat after me:

Lord, Jesus you calmed the storm on the Lake (repeat)

Calm the Storms in my life. (repeat)

Bless this water  (repeat)

that it may be a sign  (repeat)

of your love, peace, and healing. (repeat)

May we who are touched with this water (repeat)

Know your love (repeat)

through the touch of another person  (repeat)

Allow me to reach out in your love  (repeat)

Help us to reach out to our friends  (repeat)

to share this sign of your love, peace, and healing. (repeat)

Be with us Jesus. (repeat)

Amen (repeat)

As we pass the water around the circle, please make the sign of the cross on the forehead of the person to your right. Please say to that person, "May the love of Jesus bring you peace."

(*Begin playing the song,* He has Anointed Me, *Dameans or another appropriate song.*)

Take the small water container and pass it around the circle.

After all have been anointed you may wish to close with this prayer followed by a sign of peace:

"May the Lord bless us and keep us, and bring us peace until we meet again."

## Part VII

**Fellowship Time**

This is a time for winding down as well as giving and receiving support. This is a good time to share the snacks that the group brought or it may be a good time for an open gym experience.

## Journal Page 1: Jesus, Calm My Sea

Continue to talk with the Lord as you reflect on the following Journal Questions. No one will read your answers. Please reflect on the questions for your own insight.

What is my Sea like (Stormy, choppy, light chop, calm)? Explain.

_____

_____

What areas, topics, situations, people, and places cause my life to be *stormy*?

_____

_____

What areas, topics, situations, people, and places *bring quiet and calm* to my life?

_____

_____

What areas (which bring storms or calm) *do I* have control over in my life?

_____

_____

What areas (which bring storms or calm) *don't I* have control over in my life?

_____

_____

Who are the people I need to ask forgiveness of in my life?

_____

_____

Who are the people I need to forgive?

_____

_____

What strengths and good qualities do I bring to my relationships and the people in my life?  Explain.

_____

_____

What hurts have I carried around for so long, that I wish to 'lay down' and offer to the Lord today?  (Please *write* that hurt and an explanation on the strip of paper provided at the bottom of the next page. We will tear them up so no one will read them. We will ask the Lord to help us to relinquish the hurts we carry with us.)

_____

_____

Who are the people from whom I draw my strength?  Explain.

_____

_____

What places or activities of my life drain my energy, and life source?  How do I deal with this drain? Explain.

_____

_____

What people in my life drain my life energy, life source, and power?  How do I deal with this drain? Explain.

_____

_____

In what ways do the following steps fit the hurt or situation that I am dealing with?
Admit there is a hurt.
Seek counsel and come up with a workable plan to deal with the situation.
Work the plan with God's help.

_____

_____

In what ways can I begin to calm my seas with the Lord's help?

_____

_____

## Prayer

**M**y Dear Child,

I love you so much.

There is nothing that you could do,
which would separate you
from my love.

No sin is too great.
No length of time is too long.
No hurt is too painful.

Allow My love to forgive your sin,
Allow My love to close the gap of our time
apart,
Allow My love to heal the hurt which you
are feeling today.

Accept my love for you
as a child who accepts a gift
from a loving parent.

I love you.

I want to heal your hurts.
I want to calm the storms in your life.
I want to share my everlasting life
and joy with you.

But the choice is yours.

Open your heart and your hands today
as I share my love with you.
Accept my Spirit with joy
and you will see that with my help,
all things are possible.

I Am The Lord !

## Small Group Discussion

Gather in groups of 10 - 12 with a person who has volunteered to be the facilitator.

You may wish to discuss the following questions, or you may wish to discuss whatever the group members need to process at this time.

a. Was the relaxation technique helpful?

b. What did you find most helpful from the mediation experience?

c. What did you find least helpful?

d. What did you find most heplful about the witness given at the beginning of the prayer experience? How did the person's sharing of their life story help you to understand Jesus' love for you?

e. What do you ask of the Lord today that you would like to share with the group for their support in prayer? *Only share what you feel comfortable sharing.* Remember that you may 'pass'.

# So Little Time . . .

## Suggested Time

One to One and a Half Hours

## Objectives

1. To invite participants to relax in the Lord's love, peace, and healing.

2. To allow the participants time to reflect on the people in their lives who have taught them to love.

3. To invite the participants to write to those people who have been thought of in this meditation experience.

## Introduction

This meditation experience works well as an examination of relationships. Participants are invited to write to those people who have taught them to love. Forgiveness and healing may be needed in these relationships. This is a good time to ask the Lord to help in the healing process.

A personal story of how you have taken for granted the love of a parent, friend, spouse, etc. may be helpful at this point. Or you may wish to share an experience in which you have found reconciliation in a relationship. As you share your personal witness, explain how God's love helped you to begin the healing process in a relationship. You may wish to stress that the sooner the reconciliation can take place, the less time the hurt has to fester. Time tends to deepen the wound and widen the gap between those in need of forgiveness.

This experience is meant to help the participants to recognize any relationships in their lives that are in need of forgiveness.

It is important for the person giving the witness to stress that we often do not have the luxury of time to ask forgiveness and to work on healing wounds. One of the participants in our group experienced this lack of time.

Stacy, (we will call her) a senior in high school, and her father were not getting along very well. Her father had been recently diagnosed as having cancer. She was angry at her father already, because of many years of misunderstanding on both her and her father's part. Now Stacy felt that dad was abandoning her through his illness and imminent death. This only added to the hurt which she already felt. Stacy wanted to share her feelings with dad. She could not talk with him face to face, the pain was too great for her. So she wrote dad a letter telling him what she felt.

Stacy stayed up most of the night writing and crying. She poured out her love for dad in the letter. The next day Stacy asked her mom to read the letter to dad, and she left for school. That afternoon, Stacy received a phone call saying that dad was very near death and she should return home immediately. When Stacy returned home, her mom told her that she read the letter to dad and he smiled.

Stacy was present when dad died. Their relationship was healed.

At times we need to tell a loved one who has died that we are sorry for the pain that we have caused them, or just tell them that we miss them. This may be a good time to mention that those who have died still pray for us. We can 'talk with them' in prayer as we do to the saints.

It may be helpful for a person who is suffering from the death of a loved one, to write a note to the person who died. The note may be kept or it may be burned. Either way, just getting the feelings out on paper and out in prayer is very healing.

## Environment

We would like to set a relaxed and peaceful environment for this meditation.

Lights dimmed

Soft music playing (see music suggestions below)

Prayer rug set with:

Lit Incense

Lit Candle

Bible open to passage being used, 1 Peter 1:22 to 2:3 *or* Matthew 18:21-35

Olive Oil in small container(s) for anointing

Gather in circle around the Prayer rug.

## Materials

### *Participants Should bring:*

Optional:

1. Snacks for fellowship time.

2. A blanket to sit on during the meditation experience. If carpet squares are available, these may also be used. The blanket/carpet squares allow the participants to sit on the floor if they wish during the meditation experience. You may wish to have chairs available for those who wish to sit in a chair. Know the needs and the abilities of your group. The key is to help the participants to relax.

### *Leader prepares:*

Review Preparation Notes on page viii.

**Kleenex**

**Paper Towels**

**Copy Journal, page 18.**

**Copy Discussion Questions page 19.**

**Stationery** for participants to write letters to those special people who have taught them to love.

**Envelopes**

**Pens**

**Prayer Rug** (See note on page xii)

**Incense,** either drugstore/popular brand is fine or church incense may be used. See note page xii for detailed explanation.

**Candle,** (See note on page xiii)

**Scripture,** (See note on page xii-xiii)

**Olive Oil,** a few drops placed on cotton in a small container. (See note page xii for detailed explanation.)

**Record/tape player**

Ask for a volunteer or invite someone to give the witness and to introduce the theme. See Introduction page 10, and a. - e. page 13 for ideas.

Ask for a volunteer/choose adult facilitators for small group discussions. Be sure to give the discussion questions to facilitators in advance (page 19). This will help them to prepare for the discussion.

## Helpful Hints

The environment and the beginning of the meditation is similar to the first prayer experience, 'Lord, Calm My Sea'. This format is followed to help the participants to get into a comfortable routine of meditation. The more the relaxation technique is used, the less time it takes for the participants to relax.

You may wish to ask the participants to keep a prayer journal (see page x). This might be a loose leaf folder into which the participants can place the journal pages which they will be using during the meditation experiences. It is important that these pages be kept confidential. Please do not read the participants' journal pages, or ask them to read from them.

Before you begin the meditation, pass out all the materials that the participants will need.

Ask the participants to move from the circle and to sit about ten feet apart if it looks as if they might be distracted by the others sitting around them.

This meditation experience can be used with groups from 10 - 100 participants. If the group is larger than 40, you may wish to use two containers of oil for anointing. Try to work out of one circle if possible. If this is not possible, have groups of about 10 - 12 participants make circles.

In this prayer experience we will be using olive oil for the anointing. It is helpful to pour a few drops of the oil into a small container with one or two cotton balls in it. This way the cotton absorbs the oil. The person who is doing the anointing can then just touch his/her thumb on the cotton ball and moisten his/her finger with the oil. This will be used to anoint the hands of the participants.

## Music Suggestions

*Relaxation/ Meditation time*

*The Body at Prayer, Vol. 1*, St. Anthony Messenger Press, Sparough and Fisher, 1987. (Side two has ocean sounds with music.)

Or Sea Shore sounds *without* subliminal messages. (see note, pages xi, xii)

*Praise Strings Vol 11*, Maranatha! Music, 1989.

*Jonathan Livingston Sea Gull*, The Original Motion Picture Sound Track from Hall Bartlett Film, Neil Diamond, CBS Inc. 1973.

Any quiet music which will help to set the atmosphere for meditation and reflection.

## Journal time

*Times and Seasons*, Steve and Annie Chapman, 1986 Star Song Records. (The whole album is fantastic)

*Wind Beneath My Wings*, Bette Middler, from the Original Motion Picture Soundtrack "Beaches," 1988 Atlantic Recording Corp.

*The Living Years*, Mike + the Mechanics, Living Years, 1988 Atlantic Recording Corp.

*We May Never Pass This Way Again*, Seals and Crofts

*Cat's in the Cradle*, Anthology of Harry Chapin, 1985 Elektra/Asylum Records.

*You're The Only Little Girl*, *Times and Seasons*, Steve and Annie Chapman, 1986 Star Song Records.

*Reflections Vol, 1, 2, or 3*, Dameans

Any other quiet meditation music you may have access to.

## Anointing time

*He Has Anointed Me*, Dameans

## Prayer Experience at a Glance

See pages 13-17, for detailed procedure.

### Part I  (10-15 Minutes)

Gather in Circle around prayer rug.

Introduce the evening's theme, reading, and witness.

Explain the prayer rug and symbols.

### Part II  (3-5 minutes)

Pass out stationery, envelopes, pencils and journal pages.

Ask teenagers to move about ten feet apart. Adults may remain in the circle. (See note page ix)

### Part III  (20 minutes)

Relaxation / Meditation

### Part IV  (10 - 15 minutes)

Journal Experience

### Part V  (15- 20 Minutes)

*Optional:* Small Group Discussion

### Part VI  (10-15 minutes)

Closing Prayer:

Anointing

### Part VII  (10-15 minutes)

*Optional:* Fellowship, Snacks or Open Gym

### After Meditation Experience

Invite the participants to give their notes to those people who have taught them to love. Work on not taking those who love us for granted.

Continue to talk with the Lord. You may wish to encourage the participants to use the Journal as an aid to prayer.

## Evaluation / Notes

# Index

## Scripture

1 Peter 1:22 to 2:3

Matthew 18: 21-35

## Topics Discussed

Hurt, Those who have taught us to

Love, Those who have taught us to

Prayer, Introduction to

Reconciliation with:

Family

Friends

God

Time to heal relationship is often short.

## Activities

Anointing, with oil on palms of hands

Group, Large: Opening prayer Closing prayer

Group, Small: Discussion

Journal, Individual

Meditation, The Sea (a variation)

Notes written to one who has taught participants to love.

# Procedure Detailed

## Part I (10-15 Minutes)

Invite participants to Gather in Circle around prayer rug.

Introduce the evening's theme (Given by leader or by a person who can witness to the love of Jesus in their life as they have tried to reconcile themselves with another. Please mention that if hurts in relationships are not resolved soon they tend to worsen and go on being hurts carried around for a very long time.) See Introduction on page 10 as well as, questions on page 19 for idea starters.

    a. Read or paraphrase: 1 Peter 1:22 to 2:3 or Matthew 18:23-35

    b. Who are the people who have taught me to love and forgive?

    c. Those who have taught me to love have also taught me negative patterns, even though they may not have wanted to teach

me these patterns. How do we learn from other's mistakes?

    d. How have I taken time (or not taken time) to heal any hurting relationships as soon as possible?

    e. What personal insights do I have into today's theme?

Explain the prayer rug and symbols:

**Prayer Rug**, is a focal point. It will become a place upon which we set our prayer requests. We will also set items upon the rug which we will ask the Lord to bless. (See note page xii.)

**Incense**, (May already be lit or light it at this point). The incense reminds us that our prayers (like the smoke) rise up to the Lord. (See note page xii.)

**Olive Oil**, Oil was used as a means of healing in the Old and New Testament times. Oil was also used in praying for those who were in need of healing. (See note page xii.)

**Scripture**, Our focal point is God's word. We turn to the foundation and promises of the Word of God. (See note pages xii-xiii.)

**Candle**, reminds us that Jesus is the Light of the world. We call upon Jesus tonight to bring light to any areas of darkness and to bring healing to any areas of pain. (See page xiii).

## Part II (3-5 minutes)

Pass out stationery, envelopes and pencils.

Ask teenagers to move about ten feet apart. Adults may remain in the circle. (See note page ix.)

Ask participants to reflect on the following questions before we begin. They *will not* be asked to share their answers with the group.

1) Who/What gives meaning to your life?

2) Who has taught you how to love (build relationships)

    a. Good things they have taught you.

    b. Not-so-good things they have taught you.

    c. Things which you wish were different.

3) So what are you going to do? What have you learned from their mistakes?

## Part III  (20 minutes)

**Relaxation / Meditation:** (You may wish to read the script below or you may wish to adapt it to fit your needs.)

**Begin the tape:** *The Body at Prayer, Vol. 2*, St. Anthony Messenger, Sparough and Fisher, 1987. (Side two has quiet music which is great for meditation). Or any other quiet music which you would like to use.

### Relaxation  (Read/Adapt)

During this meditation experience we will work on relaxing our bodies and our minds. This will help us to reduce the distractions which usually occupy our attention. If there is a relationship which is in need of reconciliation,  I would invite you to offer it to the Lord today. Ask the Lord who forgave so many people while he walked on the Earth, to forgive you. Ask the Lord to help you to grant forgiveness to the person(s) who has hurt you.

Know that all that we do today and from this moment on will be completed in the love of Jesus. Jesus wants to forgive you and begin to heal your relationships today.

(*Speak slowly and calmly. Your voice will add to the relaxing atmosphere which you have set.*)

Try to find a *comfortable position.* You may wish to sit in the chair or on a blanket on the floor. You may even wish to lay down, but a word of caution, do not get too comfortable, since you may fall asleep.

Please *close your eyes.* This will eliminate visual distractions and will help you to focus your thoughts on the Lord.

We begin to quite our minds and bodies as we start by *slowing down our breathing.*

> As you inhale, slowly count to four without making any noise. (*Pause*)
> As you exhale, slowly count to four without making any noise.

(*Allow participants to take about 3 or 4 breaths and continue.*)

> As you inhale accept the Spirit of God into your life. (*Pause*)
> As you exhale let go of anything which makes you nervous or anxious.

(*Allow participants to take about 3 or 4 breaths and continue.*)

As your breathing slows and calms, so will your body and mind.

(*Speak slowly and calmly. Your voice will add to the relaxing atmosphere which you have set.*)

Our next step in relaxation will be relaxing various muscle groups.

Beginning with your *forehead,* crinkle it up and close your *eyes* as tightly as you can. Feel the tension in your forehead, the corners of your eyes, and feel your nose crinkle up. Hold the tension . . . and then relax. Feel what it is like to be tense and relaxed.

Then hold your *lips* together as tightly as you can and *bite down* as hard as you can. Feel the tension in the corners of your mouth and in your jaw. Hold the tension . . . and then relax. Feel what it is like to be tense and relaxed.

> As you inhale, slowly count to four without making any noise. (*Pause*)
> As you exhale, slowly count to four without making any noise.

(*Allow participants to take about 3 or 4 breaths and continue.*)

> As you inhale accept the Spirit of God into your life. (*Pause*)
> As you exhale let go of anything which makes you nervous or anxious.

(*Allow participants to take about 3 or 4 breaths and continue.*)

Next, we will work on relaxing your *neck.* Allow your chin to touch your chest and begin to slowly do some neck rolls. First to the right . . . Feel the tension as you extend various muscles . . . Then go to the left . . . and begin to work out the kinks  in your neck. Now return your head to a resting position and relax. Feel what it is like to be tense and relaxed.

Now, Shrug your *shoulders.* Move them as close to your neck as you can. Feel the tension in your neck and shoulders. Then push your shoulders toward your feet. Move them away from your neck. Feel the tension under your arms, in your back and in your neck. Hold the tension . . . and then relax. Feel what it is like to be tense and relaxed.

> As you inhale, remember to count slowly to four. (*Pause*)
> As you exhale, remember to count slowly to four.

(*Allow participants to take about 3 or 4 breaths and continue.*)

As you inhale accept the Spirit of God into your life. (*Pause*)
As you exhale let go of anything which makes you nervous or anxious.

(*Allow participants to take about 3 or 4 breaths and continue.*)

Beginning with your right hand, make a fist and tighten up all the muscles in your *right arm*, forearm and biceps. Feel the tension in your right arm. Hold the tension. You may even feel your right arm quiver. Experience the tension . . . and then relax. Feel what it is like to be tense and relaxed.

Now repeat the same procedure with your Left hand. Make a fist and tighten up all the muscles in your *left arm*, forearm and biceps. Feel the tension in your Left arm. Hold the tension. You may even feel your Left arm quiver . . . and then relax. Feel what it is like to be tense and relaxed.

As you inhale, remember to count slowly to four. (*Pause*)
As you exhale, remember to count slowly to four.

(*Allow participants to take about 3 or 4 breaths and continue.*)

As you inhale accept the Spirit of God into your life. (*Pause*)
As you exhale let go of anything which makes you nervous or anxious.

(*Allow participants to take about 3 or 4 breaths and continue.*)

Beginning with your *right leg*. Curl up your foot and tighten all the muscles in your right leg, calf and thigh. Feel the tension in your right leg. Hold the tension. You may even feel your right leg quiver and be on the verge of a cramp. Experience the tension . . . and now relax. Feel what it is like to be tense and relaxed.

Now repeat the same procedure with your *left leg*. Curl up your foot and tighten all the muscles in your Left leg, calf and thigh. Feel the tension in your Left leg. Hold the tension. You may even feel your Left leg quiver and becoming on the verge of a cramp . . . and now relax. Feel what it is like to be tense and relaxed.

Tighten your abdomen muscles as you inhale, and allow the tension to leave you as you exhale.

Now that your body is calm and relaxed, I would ask you to think about your favorite beach.

## Meditation

(*Pause after each question.*)

First we will focus on the sky.

What colors are the sky?
Are there clouds?
What position is the Sun? Morning, afternoon, evening? Maybe night time?
What do you see that you have never noticed before?

Next we will focus on the water.

What does the water look like?
What colors are present?
Is the water calm or choppy?
What does the water smell like?
What do you see that you have never noticed before?

Finally we will focus on the beach itself.

Now look at the beach around you?
What is in or on the sand around you?
What do you see that you have never noticed before?

Pick up a handful of sand and look at it. What do you see that you have never noticed before?

I would ask you at this point to walk into the water until you are about waste deep. Keep looking out to sea.

If the waves are choppy, they may try to push you back. As you enter the water, begin to notice that with each breath that you take, the waves will begin to quiet until they finally become calm.

Invite Jesus on to your beach. As you turn around, Jesus is standing behind you on the shore.

What do his eyes look like?
What does his face look like?
How tall is he?

What do you feel as you look at him and as he extends a hand toward you?

Jesus invites you to leave the water. As you come out of the water, Jesus embraces you. What do you tell him that you have wanted to tell him for so long, but you have never had the time to before? And what is his response to you?

What are the things which make the Lord 'Proud' of you?

Do you know that you could never lose or win the Lord's love? God loves you just the way you are.

Jesus tells you that you could never win or lose his love for you. He loves you because you are you!

Talk with the Lord about what is important to your relationship today.

*(Pause after each paragraph.)*

Jesus asks you to invite the person who has taught you to love onto your beach.

As this special person walks toward you down the beach, what emotion do you experience?

What do this person's eyes look like?
What does this person's face look like?
How tall is this person?

Jesus embraces this person who holds such a tender spot in your heart.

What do you feel as you look at Jesus and this important person?

Jesus invites you to join him and your special guest. As you walk toward Jesus, he brings you both together in Loving arms.

What do you tell this important person in your life, that you have wanted to tell him/her for so long, but you have never had the time or courage to tell them before? And what is his/her response to you?

What are the things which make this person 'Proud' of you?

Do you know that you could never lose or win this person's love? God and this person love you just the way you are.

What hurts need to be healed in your relationship with this person?

Ask the Lord to bring healing to your relationship.

As Jesus continues to embrace your friend and yourself on the beach, open your eyes. Take the risk of writing that special person a note. Tell them what they mean to you. The questions on the journal page may help you in writing your letter. If the person is deceased, still write the note and place it in the envelope.

Please write the letter even if you do not want to give it to them. The process of writing is very healing when it is done in the Lord's presence. It helps us to begin the healing process.

## Part IV  (15 - 20 minutes)

Journal Experience (page 18)

(Play the songs: )

*Times and Seasons*, Steve and Annie Chapman (The whole album is fantastic)

*Wind Beneath My Wings*,

*We May Never Pass This Way Again*, Seals and Crofts

*Cat's in the Cradle*, Harry Chapin

*You're The Only Little Girl*, Times and Seasons, Steve and Annie Chapman

Any other quiet meditation music you may have access to.

## Part V  (15- 20 Minutes)

Optional: Small Group Discussion (see notes page viii)

Gather in groups of 10 - 12 with a person who has volunteered to be the facilitator.

You may wish to discuss:

a. Was the relaxation technique helpful? Why/why not?

b. What did you find the most helpful about the meditation/journal experience?

c. What did you find the least helpful about the meditation/journal experience?

d. What do you ask of the Lord today? Share only what you feel comfortable sharing or what you want the group to pray for?

e. Did the journal questions help in understanding a relationship better? Why/why not?

f. Did you write the note to the person who was in need of forgiving or from whom you needed to ask forgiveness ? Why/why not?

g. Those who have taught us to love have also taught us negative patterns, even though they may not have wanted to teach us these patterns. How do we take the positive qualities of what we have learned and try to leave the negative with some wisdom from these experiences?

h. Why is it important to take the time to heal any hurting relationships as soon as possible?

i. What did you find most helpful in the witness given at the beginning of the prayer experience?

## Part VI (10-15 minutes)

Closing Prayer:

(*Before you regather in the circle, ask participants to:*)

### Option A

Write the name of the person you wish to give the letter to on the envelope. As we gather in the circle, please place the sealed envelope in the basket on the prayer rug. The envelopes *will be given back at the end of the closing prayer.*

### Option B

(*If the group has about 20 participants, pass the basket and place the envelopes in the basket.*)

Please write the person's name on the front of the envelope. They will be returned at the end of the closing prayer.

If you would like to place your envelope in the basket and share with the group what you would like the group to pray for in regards to this relationship, please share your petition.

If you would like to place your envelope in the basket silently, please do that. Know that we are still praying for your request as you silently place your envelope in the basket.

(*Pause for collection of envelopes. You may wish to play some quiet music.*)

### Regather in Circle.

(*When the envelopes have been placed on the prayer rug the following may be said.*)

We have met the Lord in three ways today . . .

In the meditation and journal time.

In the discussion and small group sharing.

And now in the touch of another person.

We will now pray over the letters and the oil.

Please hold out your right hand and we will ask the Lord to bless these letters which are written out of love. Please repeat after me.

Lord, you are Father and Mother to each of us (Repeat)

You are the source of all love, forgiveness, and healing. (*Repeat*)

Bless those who have taught us to love. (Repeat)

Help us to forgive them for the negative things they have taught us. (Repeat)

Help us to ask forgiveness for the hurts that we have caused them. (Repeat)

We ask that these letters of love (Repeat)
   bring your love, healing, and peace (Repeat)
   to our relationships. (Repeat)

(*Pause*)

We ask you to bless this oil Lord. (Repeat)

May it be a sign (Repeat)
   of your love, peace, and healing. (Repeat)

May we who are touched with this oil (Repeat)
   know your love (Repeat)
   through the touch of another. (Repeat)

Allow us to reach out in your love (Repeat)
   as we reach out to our friends and loved ones (Repeat)
   with this sign of your love, peace, and healing. (Repeat)

Be with us always, (Repeat)

Amen. (Repeat)

(*Take the small oil container.*)

Now please make the Sign of the Cross on the person's palms to the right of you. By doing this, we ask the Lord to bless our hands that we may bring healing and forgiveness to those people in our lives.

Please say the following as you anoint their palms, "May your hands bring the loving forgiveness of Jesus to everyone in your life." (*Or you may wish to say prayer*)

(*Begin the song,* He Has Anointed Me, *Dameans*)

(*When the anointing is finished say*)

May the Lord of love and forgiveness guide us and hold us safely in the palm of her hand until we gather again in her love. Amen.

Please give the letter to the person at a time when they can read it with out distractions. You may wish to place it on their night stand, or pillow before bedtime.

Be sure to pick up your envelope before you leave.

## Part VII (10-15 minutes)

Fellowship time or open gym

## Journal Page: *So Little Time . . .*

*Please answer the journal questions honestly. These will help you in writing your letter.*

Reflect on the following questions. Please write or reflect on your answers. You will not be asked to share their answers with the group.

You may wish to tell them in a note . . .

You may wish to begin by remembering the questions which you have reflected on at the beginning of the meditation.

1) Who/What gives meaning to your life?

2) Who has taught you how to love (build relationships)?

    a. Good things they have taught you.
    b. Not-so-good things they have taught you.
    c. Things which you wish were different.

3) So what are you going to do? What have you learned from their mistakes?

*How has your relationship gone through the following cycle? Identify various times in your relationship that you have experienced the cycle below.*

Relationships often move through a cycle of:

    a) 'Easy to Love'
    b) 'Difficult to Love'
    c) 'I Love You More Today Then Yesterday'

How has your relationship passed through this cycle? Explain.

*In your note you may wish to:*

• Thank them for teaching you how to love.

• Tell them something you've always wanted to tell them, but have never had the time or courage to tell them before.

• Thank this person for the good times in your relationship, as well as those not so good times which you both have survived and grown through. Be as honest as you can be.

• Ask forgiveness, or even tell this person that they are forgiven.

Give this person your letter at a quiet time. Place it on their pillow so they will read it before bed. Give it to them when they are quiet and not hurried. Mail it to them if they live far away.

## Facilitator's Copy

### Small Group Discussion

You may wish to discuss the questions below or whatever else the group needs to process at this time.

a. Was the relaxation technique helpful? Why, why not?

b. What did you find the most helpful about the meditation/journal experience? Why?

c. What did you find the least helpful about the meditation/journal experience? Why?

d. What do you ask of the Lord tonight? Share only what you feel comfortable sharing or what you want the group to pray for.

e. Did the journal questions help in understanding a relationship better? Why? Why not?

f. Did you write the note to the person who was in need of forgiving or from whom you needed to ask forgiveness? Share only what you feel comfortable, if you feel comfortable sharing anything. Why? Why not?

g. Those who have taught us to love have also taught us negative patterns, even though they may not have wanted to teach us these patterns. How do we take the positive qualities of what we have learned and try to leave the negative with some wisdom from these experiences?

h. Why is it important to take the time to heal any hurting relationships as soon as possible?

i. What did you find most helpful in the witness given at the beginning of the prayer experience?

# Reconciliation

## Suggested Time

One hour to one hour and a half.

## Objectives

1. To help participants to relax in the Lord's love, peace, and healing.

2. To invite participants to ask the Lord to be with them when they are tempted in a familiar situation in which they sin.

3. To invite participants to complete a journal page which will help them to prepare for reconciliation.

## Introduction

The meditation/prayer experience invites the participants to relax—body and mind. The participants are invited to ask Jesus to be their strength when they are at their weakest point and are tempted to sin.

Often times we separate 'sacred' and 'non-sacred' times. This meditation helps the participants to know that Jesus is with them always.

We can draw on the strength of Jesus when we are at our weakest.

The person giving the introduction may wish to share a personal story of how he/she has relied on the Lord's strength when he/she was at their lowest point. This will help the participants to experience God's love as he/she witnesses to it.

Allow the participants to process what is going on in their lives. Ask the Lord to be present as the healing process begins or continues for the participants in your life.

Focus on how we need to accept the responsibilities of being a Christian for ourselves. We need to ask forgiveness for the times we have sinned. This helps us to restore relationships which have suffered from the sins we have committed, or those which another has committed that have hurt us.

By asking or granting forgiveness, we can then begin to examine how we can break the negative patterns which have developed in our lives.

You (or the person giving the introduction) may wish to talk about how you have overcome negative patterns in your own life. How did you recognize the patterns, and then with Jesus' help and love, overcome these destructive patterns?

We will conclude today, by renewing our baptismal promises and accepting God's love in a very special way.

Be honest in your sharing and ask the Holy Spirit to speak through your words to the hearts of those who are listening.

This experience can be used to prepare the participants for the Sacrament of Reconciliation during the hour and a half time period, or you may suggest that the participants receive the sacrament on their own. Either way, be sure to explain why reception of the Sacrament of Reconciliation is important in Catholic Theology.

## Environment

A relaxed atmosphere in which the participants are freed from as many distractions as possible, will work best.

Lights dimmed.

Soft music playing when participants enter the room (see suggestions below).

Prayer rug set with:

Lit incense

Lit candle

Bible Open to the passage being used (see suggestions)

Water in small containers for each small group.

Basket/Bag to collect prayer requests

*Materials*

Participants Should Bring:

Optional:

Snacks for fellowship time.

A blanket to sit on during the meditation experience.

*Leader Prepares:*

Review of Preparation Notes on page vi.

**Kleenex**

**Copy Journal pages** (28, 29)

**Stationary** for participants to write a letter to the person that is in need of forgiveness in their lives.

**Pens**

**Envelopes**

**Stationary for writing letters** (page 28)

**Crayons**

**Journal Pages**

**Prayer Rug**

**Incense**

**Containers for water** (one for each small group)

**Baskets for collecting petitions.** Have one for each small group. (See page xiii for a more detailed explanation.)

**Candle for each small group.** (See page xiii for a more detailed explanation.)

**Record/tape player.**

Choose/ask for a volunteer to give a witness on how the love of Jesus has helped him/her to grant or receive forgiveness. See Introduction on page 20 for insights on the Introduction.

Choose/ask for volunteers for small (10-12 participants) group facilitators. It would be helpful to copy the questions for the small group discussion page 30) and give them the copies well in advance. Discuss the role of facilitator in the closing service. Allow facilitator to look over the service in advance.

Groups may be assigned by name tags, or may be random by asking participants to gather into groups of 10-12.

Copies of discussion questions page 30 for the small group leaders as well as closing prayer service on pages 26, 27.

# Helpful Hints

As it has been mentioned in previous prayer experiences, you may wish to ask the participants to keep a prayer journal. This might be a loose leaf folder into which the participants can place the journal pages which they will be using during the meditation experiences. It is important that these pages be kept confidential. Please do not read the participants' journal pages, or ask them to read from them. (See note page x)

Before you begin the meditation, pass out all the journal materials that the participants will need.

Ask the participants to move from the circle and sit about ten feet apart if it looks as if they might be distracted by the others sitting around them.

This meditation experience can be used with groups from 10 - 200 participants. If the group is larger than 40, you may wish to use more than one candle, container of water for anointing, and one basket to collect petitions for each small group. (See notes page xiii)

# Music Suggestions

*Relaxation/Meditation Time*

You may wish to use songs from the prayer experience, *So Little Time.* See suggestions on page 12.

*The Body at Prayer, Vol. 1*, Using Your Body in Prayer, St. Anthony Messenger Press, Sparough and Fisher, 1987. (Side two has ocean sounds with music.)

Or Sea Shore sounds *without* subliminal messages.

*Praise Strings, Vol 11*, Maranatha! Music, 1989.

*Jonathan Livingston Sea Gull*, The Original Motion Picture Sound Track from the Hall Bartlett Film, Neil Diamond, CBS Inc. 1973.

*Closing Prayer*

Continue to play soft instrumental music.

## Prayer Experience at a Glance

See pages 22-26, for detailed procedure.

### Part I (10-15 Minutes)

Gather in Circle around prayer rug

Introduce the evening's theme and share reading

Explain the prayer rug and symbols

### Part II (3-5 minutes)

Pass out pens, stationary, envelopes and journal pages.

Ask teenagers to move about ten feet apart. Adults may remain in the circle. (See note page ix)

### Part III (20 minutes)

Relaxation/Meditation

### Part IV (10-15 minutes)

Journal Experience

Participants may individually receive the Sacrament of Reconciliation from this time on to the end of the prayer experience.

### Part V (10-15 minutes)

Small groups of 10-12 sharing of insights

Placing petitions in Basket

Recommitment to Baptismal Promises

Anointing with water by adult leader in small group

### After Meditation Experience

Give notes to person in need of forgiveness.

Seek counseling for specific need.

Prepare for reception of the Sacrament of Reconciliation if not received at this time.

## Evaluation/Notes

## Scripture: Index

John 8:2-11

John 9:1-7

Matthew 18:21-35

Luke 4:1-13

Psalm 51

### Topics Discussed: Index

Baptismal Promises renewed.

Examination of Conscience

Forgiveness, finding peace and strength with God

Forgiveness, Asking for

Negative patterns, breaking the cycle of

Reconciliation: Family, Friends, God

Reconciliation, Preparation for Sacrament

Small group discussion

Temptation, turning away with Jesus' help

### Activities: Index

Anointing: with water on forehead

Baptismal Promises, Renewal of

Group, large, opening prayer

Group, small, closing prayer, discussion

Journal, Individual reflection time

Note to a person(s) who is in need of forgiveness or who need to be asked forgiveness.

Note to yourself seeking forgiveness and asking God's help.

Meditation, 'your favorite spot to be alone'

Petitions: written, ripped up, placed in basket

## Procedure Detailed

### Part I (10-15 Minutes)

Invite participants to gather in a circle around prayer rug.

Introduce the prayer experience theme (Given by leader or a person who can witness to the love of Jesus which has brought reconciliation to their life. Focus on how the Lord helped this person to be freed of the temptation that they had been, and possibly still are, dealing with.) See Introduction on page 20, and discussion questions on page 30, for idea starters.

a. Share one of the scripture readings. (See options page 22.)

b. Need to identify areas in my life which are in need of healing.

c. I know that the Lord has forgiven me for any sins I have committed.

d. I know that the Lord is with me every minute of the day. God's love and strength is there for me to draw on if I only accept it.

e. How do I reach out in the Lord's love and share the Lord's healing and forgiveness with those in my daily life?

f. We will renew our baptismal promises and recommit our lives to the Lord.

g. If this is preparation for the Sacrament of Reconciliation, it would be a good idea to talk about the need for the formal Sacrament of Reconciliation.

Explain the prayer rug and symbols:

**Prayer Rug:** becomes a focal point in the center of the circle. (See note page xii.)

**Scripture:** the center of all that we do in our lives and in our prayers. The scriptures tell us how Jesus loved and cared for the people of his time and how he loves and cares for each of us today. (See note page xii-xiii.)

**Incense:** (may already be lit or you may wish to light it at this point.) A sign that our prayers rise before the Lord just as the smoke rises. (See note page xii.)

**Water:** reminds us of our baptism. When we were baptized others promised that we would reject sin and follow the Lord. At this time we recommit ourselves to the Lord and once again reject sin to follow the Lord. Use water taken from the baptismal fountain for this prayer experience. (See note page xii.)

**Candle:** this reminds us that Jesus is the Light of the world. We gather around this light tonight and ask the Lord to bring Light and love to any areas of darkness and sin in our lives. (See note page xiii.)

**Basket:** this will be used to collect the prayer requests that the participants have concerning reconciliation. This will help in the 'letting go' process of holding onto sin, hurt, and pain and will give way to forgiveness, healing and health. (See note page xiii.)

## Part II (3-5 minutes)

Pass out pens, stationary, envelopes and journal pages.

Ask teenagers to move about ten feet apart. Adults may remain in the circle. (See note page ix.)

## Part III (20 minutes)

Relaxation

*(You may wish to read the script below or you may wish to adapt to fit your needs.)*

*Begin the tape,* The Body at Prayer, *Vol. 2, St. Anthony Messenger, Sparough and Fisher, 1987. (Side two which has quiet reflection music). Or any other quiet reflection type music* without *subliminal messages. (See pages xi, xii)*

During this workshop we will work on relaxing our bodies and our minds. This will help us to reduce the distractions which usually occupy our attention. If there is a need of forgiveness in your life, ask the Lord to bring forgiveness and healing to this today. Ask the Lord, who forgave sinners as he walked upon the earth and healed those who were in need of healing, to grant your request today.

Know that all that we do from this moment on will be completed with Jesus at our side. We do everything in Jesus' name and love.

*(Speak slowly and calmly. Your voice will add to the relaxing atmosphere which you have set.)*

Try to find *comfortable position.* You may wish to sit in the chair or on a blanket on the floor. You may even wish to lay down, but a word of caution, do not get too comfortable, since you may fall asleep.

Please *close your eyes.* This will eliminate visual distractions and will help you to focus your thoughts on the Lord.

As we begin to quiet our minds and bodies as we start by *slowing down our breathing.*

As you inhale, slowly count to four without making any noise. *(Pause)*

As you exhale, slowly count to four without making any noise.

*(Allow participants to take about 3 or 4 breaths and continue.)*

As you inhale accept the Spirit of God into your life. *(Pause)*

As you exhale let go of anything which makes you nervous or anxious.

(*Allow participants to take about 3 or 4 breaths and continue.*)

As your breathing slows and calms, so will your body and mind.

(*Speak slowly and calmly. Your voice will add to the relaxing atmosphere which you have set.*)

Our next step in relaxation will be *relaxing various muscle groups.*

Beginning with your *forehead*, crinkle it up and close your *eyes* as tightly as you can. Feel the tension in your forehead, the corners of your eyes, and feel your nose crinkle up. Hold the tension . . . and then relax. Feel what it is like to be tense and relaxed.

Then hold your *lips* together as tightly as you can and *bite down* as hard as you can. Feel the tension in the corners of your mouth and in your jaw. Hold the tension . . . and then relax. Feel what it is like to be tense and relaxed.

As you inhale, slowly count to four without making any noise. (*Pause*)

As you exhale, slowly count to four without making any noise.

(*Allow participants to take about 3 or 4 breaths and continue.*)

As you inhale accept the Spirit of God into your life. (*Pause*)

As you exhale let go of anything which makes you nervous or anxious.

(*Allow participants to take about 3 or 4 breaths and continue.*)

Next, we will work on relaxing your *neck*. Allow you chin to touch your chest and begin to slowly do some neck rolls. First to the right . . . Feel the tension as you extend various muscles . . . Then go to the left . . . and begin to work out the kinks in your neck. Now return your head to a resting position and relax. Feel what it is like to be tense and relaxed.

Now, Shrug your *shoulders*. Move them as close to your neck as you can. Feel the tension in your neck and shoulders. Then push your shoulders toward your feet. Move them away from your neck. Feel the tension under your arms, in your back and in your neck. Hold the tension . . . and then relax. Feel what it is like to be tense and relaxed.

As you inhale, remember to count slowly to four. (*Pause*)

As you exhale, remember to count slowly to four.

(*Allow participants to take about 3 or 4 breaths and continue.*)

As you inhale accept the Spirit of God into your life. (*Pause*)

As you exhale let go of anything which makes you nervous or anxious.

(*Allow participants to take about 3 or 4 breaths and continue.*)

Beginning with your right hand, make a fist and tighten up all the muscles in your *right arm*, forearm and biceps. Feel the tension in your right arm. Hold the tension. You may even feel your right arm quiver. Experience the tension . . . and then relax. Feel what it is like to be tense and relaxed.

Now repeat the same procedure with your Left hand. Make a fist and tighten up all the muscles in your *left arm*, forearm and biceps. Feel the tension in your Left arm. Hold the tension. You may even feel your Left arm quiver . . . and then relax. Feel what it is like to be tense and relaxed.

As you inhale, remember to count slowly to four. (*Pause*)

As you exhale, remember to count slowly to four.

(*Allow participants to take about 3 or 4 breaths and continue.*)

As you inhale accept the Spirit of God into your life. (*Pause*)

As you exhale let go of anything which makes you nervous or anxious.

(*Allow participants to take about 3 or 4 breaths and continue.*)

Beginning with your *right leg.* Curl up your foot and tighten all the muscles in your right leg, calf and thigh. Feel the tension in your right leg. Hold the tension. You may even feel your right leg quiver and be on the verge of a cramp. Experience the tension . . . and now relax. Feel what it is like to be tense and relaxed.

Now repeat the same procedure with your *left leg.* Curl up your foot and tighten all the muscles in your Left leg, and thigh. Feel the tension in your Left leg.

Hold the tension. You may even feel your Left leg quiver and becoming on the verge of a cramp . . . and now relax. Feel what it is like to be tense and relaxed.

Tighten your abdomen muscles as you inhale, and allow the tension to leave you as you exhale.

(*Pause between each paragraph.*)

Think of your favorite place to be alone.

Be as specific as possible as you visualize your favorite place to be alone.

What do you see close to you?

Look around you . . . What is in front of you . . . to your right . . . to your left . . . and behind you.
Try to notice as many details as possible.

What do you see farther away from you?

Look around you . . . In front . . . to your right . . . to your left . . . and behind you.
Try to notice as many details as possible.

What do you see above you?

What do you see below you?

Once again, try to notice as many details as possible.

Invite Jesus to be with you in this quiet place.

What feelings do you experience as Jesus enters this quiet place?

Look at Jesus' face. Look into his eyes. Tell him what you need forgiveness of and what you wish Jesus to do for you today.

Tell the Lord who the person or persons are that you need to ask forgiveness.

(*Longer Pause*)

What sin are you in need of forgiveness?

Which sin is the most common that you deal with?

Think about the situation that is present when you are tempted to commit this sin.

Now think about the environment or chain of events which usually lead up to you committing the sin.

Picture Jesus sitting next to you or embracing you or holding your hand as you enter this environment; this chain of events which usually leads up to you committing the sin.

Look deep into Jesus eyes. Tell him what you are tempted to do. Tell the Lord what it is that you would like him to do for you.

What Does Jesus say to you?

Listen to the compassion and love in Jesus' voice as he tells you that he wishes to relieve the pain of this temptation. He wishes to relieve the feelings of failure and emptiness that accompanies this action.

Now imagine the event or chain of events as they begin. Remember that Jesus is beside you, protecting you, and giving you strength to say "NO!" to the temptation.

As this time of temptation unfolds, as it has so many times before, Jesus is with you bringing you peace and giving you courage. Jesus helps you to say "NO!" to this temptation. Turn to Jesus and look into the Lord's eyes. You are given the strength to say "NO!" to the temptation.

(*Longer Pause*)

Jesus brings forgiveness and healing to your memory as well as your physical body. He embraces you and forgives you of your sins.

Who are the people you have hurt by your sin? They may be people you know or faceless, unknown people. Either way your sin still effects them. Picture those people your sin has hurt standing near Jesus.

Jesus walks over to the person or persons whom you have hurt in this situation. Jesus embraces each person.

Look at Jesus' face and the face of the person Jesus embraces. (*Pause*)

What does Jesus say to that person and what does that person say to Jesus? (*Pause*)

Look at the emotion in Jesus' face as he embraces this person.

Jesus embraces the person who hurt you or whom you have hurt by your sin. Jesus brings them healing and asks them to forgive you.

Jesus invites you to join him and each person you have hurt. Jesus' arms come around you and each person that you have hurt, one at a time.

What do you tell each person, that you have wanted to tell them for a long time, but you may not have had the courage, or the time, or the strength to tell them before? What is their response?

Jesus does the same for each person you have invited into this meditation. (*Longer Pause*)

Jesus places his arm around you. You both walk away from this experience renewed, refreshed, and transformed. You return to the quiet place where we began this meditation.

As you walk with Jesus, talk with him about how you will see the people you once had trouble with in a new light. How will you tell them that you are sorry for the pain that you have cause them?

Please open your eyes and continue your prayer experience as you complete the journal pages.

## Part IV (10-15 minutes)

Journal Experience (28, 29)

Continue with quiet music.

Invite participants to receive the Sacrament of Reconciliation at this point if you wish to include the Sacrament in the prayer experience.

## Part V (10-15 minutes)

See notes pages x-xi for small group discussion.

Gather in small groups of 10-12.

---

# Closing Prayer

*Participants Remain in small groups.*

(The Leader invites the Adult Facilitators and youth helpers to gather around the prayer rug. Entire large groups (still sitting in their small group circles) prays for the adult facilitators:

### Option A

As the leader does a 'Laying on of Hands' for each facilitator. Ask the entire large group, "Please pray for each faciltator. Ask the Lord to help this person to be open to the Spirit and to allow the Spirit to flow through them. Focus your prayer on each facilitator, one at a time."

### Option B

Ask participants to hold out their right hands toward the facilitators and youth helpers. Ask participants to pray quietly for them that they may be Pipelines of God's love.

(Read/Adapt)

We have met Jesus in meditation, Journal, and in discussion. We will now reach out to each other in Jesus' love.

Today we will renew our baptismal vows—the promises that our parents and God parents made for

us. I invite you to ask the Lord to be with you in every step of your daily journey, every moment of your life.

Please hold out your right hand and pray over the holy water taken from the Baptismal Fountain with me.

Please repeat after me . . .

Lord Jesus, (Repeat)

You died that I might have life. (Repeat)

Your blood has washed away my sins. (Repeat)

Stand with me, Lord. (Repeat)

Be with me always. (Repeat)

Help me to turn away from sin (Repeat)

And to turn toward you (Repeat)

(*Pause*)

Bless this water, Lord (Repeat)

That we who are touched with this water (Repeat)

Will know your forgiveness, peace and healing in our hearts (Repeat)

Wash your Spirit over us (Repeat)

Fill us with your Spirit (Repeat)

Amen! (Repeat)

Adult facilitator returns to small group and leads the closing service today in the small group. He/she brings water from the prayer rug.

### Option A:

You may wish to have a chair at the center of each small group circle. Ask the participants to sit in the center of the circle. The facilitator will then do the anointing at the center of the circle. He/she may wish to do a laying on of hands at this point. See page xi for notes on laying on of hands.

The leader may use the closing prayer as found above.

### Option B:

(*Have participants remain in the circle. Facilitators will go up to each participant as they sit in the Circle.*)

Please rip up your petition of forgiveness. One by one, place your petitions in the basket. Then I will ask you the questions that your Godparents were asked to answer for you at your baptism.

I will then make the Sign of the Cross on your forehead with the water from the baptismal fountain.

(*The leader then goes to each member in the group. (A) He/she may invite participants to sit in the chair at the center of the circle, or (B) May go from person to person as they sit in the circle.*)

The participant then places his/her prayer request in the basket after they have ripped it up.

The leader then asks the participant the following questions:

A. Do you reject sin so that you can live in the freedom of god's children?

B. Do you reject the glamour of evil, and refuse to be mastered by sin?

C. Do you reject Satan, the father of sin and the prince of darkness?

(*The leader then makes the Sign of the Cross on the participants forehead and says,*)

D. May the love of Jesus break the cycle of sin and bring you forgiveness and healing.

An embrace may be an appropriate gesture following the anointing.

It would help to keep everyone in their groups until all the other groups have finished the closing prayer. This will cut down on distractions from those who finish early.

# Small Group Questions

*Reconciliation*

a. What insights did you gain from the witness and introduction to the prayer experience?

b. What do I find most difficult about forgiving myself? (Explain what you feel comfortable sharing.)

c. What do I find most difficult about forgiving another person? (Explain what you feel comfortable sharing.)

d. What do I find most difficult about asking another person to forgive me? (Explain what you feel comfortable sharing.)

e. What do I find most difficult about asking God's forgiveness? (Explain what you feel comfortable sharing.)

f. Do you really feel forgiven when you ask for God's forgiveness? (Explain what you feel comfortable sharing.)

g. Is there any sin which God would not forgive? (Explain what you feel comfortable sharing.)

h. Any other feelings about tonight's experience

i. What were the promises that you made at your baptism? (See page 27 A-D.)

## Reconciliation I

No one will read this but you. You will not be asked to share anything from this paper with the group. Please be as honest in your reflections as possible.

Sometimes it is easy to break negative patterns of behavior other times we need help.

In what ways do the following steps fit the situation of sin or negative behavior patterns that I am dealing with?

* Admit there is a hurt.
* Seek counsel and come up with a workable plan to deal with the situation.
* Work the plan with God's help.

Short term/long term goals for taking care of neglected areas of my life.

Short term/long term goals for correcting some of the dilemmas that I have actively caused.

## Reconciliation II

What is the most difficult offense for me to forgive? Why?

What is the most difficult offense for me to ask forgiveness for? Why?

Who is the most difficult person for me to forgive? Why?

Who is the most difficult person to ask forgiveness from? Why?

Areas I have neglected to take care of in my life (areas that I have control of)? Why?

Areas that I have actively 'messed-up' (that I have control over)? Why?

What do I need to forgive myself for? Why?

Here is time to write a note to myself asking for or granting forgiveness from myself. I am often the hardest on myself and refuse to allow God to heal my hurts and forgive my failings.

Here is time to write a note to the person I need to forgive. Paper is available for this.

Here is some time to write a note to the Lord. What do you wish to say to the Lord right now?

*Draw a Picture of you and the Lord as you resist the tempation that you face together.*
*Turn from the temptation and turn to the Lord.*

## Tear Off

Please tear this off and place it in the basket at the end of the prayer service.

*No one* will read this. Please be as honest as possible, we will destroy them at the end of the prayer service.

What hurt have you caused another through your sin? How will you ask forgiveness from this person?

## Small Group Questions

a. What insights did you gain from the witness and introduction to the prayer experience?

b. What do I find most difficult about forgiving myself?

c. What do I find most difficult about forgiving another person?

d. What do I find most difficult about asking another person to forgive me?

e.  What do I find most difficult about asking God's forgiveness?

f. Do I really feel forgiven when asking for God's forgiveness?

g. What were the promises that you made at your baptism? (See page 27.)

h. Any other feelings about tonight's experience?

i. Is there any sin which God would not forgive?

Remain in small groups.